1291017

TEAMWORK
Post Office

Philippa Perry and Stephen Gibbs

Wayland

Imprint details are on page 31.

Coder
Tony Allen
(pages 15–16)

NP 4000 operator
Fred Leader
(pages 17–18)

Contents

The History of the Post

Hail the mail

In about 27 BC the Roman Emperor, Augustus Caesar, set up a postal system which was similar to the one we use today.

The system worked very like a relay race. Messengers on horseback rode about the empire, using the well-built Roman roads. When the horses tired, they could stop at one of the specially built 'post houses' that were sited throughout the empire. They were called post houses because they tied their horses to the posts outside. Another messenger would be waiting there with fresh horses to take the mail to the next stage of the journey.

The messengers delivered some private mail as well as official documents. But when the Roman Empire collapsed in AD 476, the postal system disappeared for over a thousand years.

Penny Post

The London Penny Post was set up in 1680 by a merchant called William Dockwra. He delivered mail anywhere in London for a fixed price of one penny.

The British government quickly realized what a good system this was and took it over for the rest of the country. In the 1780s mailcoaches were set up to carry both post and passengers across the country.

▲ In the 1700s, mailcoaches like this one carried post and passengers from town to town.

▲ Rowland Hill – the inventor of the postage stamp.

Fact-file
- Britain is the only country in the world whose stamps show no mention of the country they come from.
- Highwaymen, such as the famous Dick Turpin, robbed mailcoaches during the 1700s.
- The highest price ever paid for a stamp was £1,350,000 for a Penny Black dated 2 May 1840.
- The oldest post-box dates from 1690. It can be found at the White Hart coaching inn in Spilsby, Lincolnshire.

Penny Black

Until 1840 the cost of posting a letter was always paid for by the person receiving the letter rather than the person sending it. Sometimes people refused to pay to accept a letter!

Then, on 1 May 1840, the postage stamp was introduced. People sending a letter had to buy a stamp first and fix it to the envelope. The idea was thought up by Rowland Hill, a retired schoolteacher. The first stamps were called Penny Blacks. The reason for this was simple: they were printed in black ink and cost one penny.

Before long every country in the world was copying Rowland Hill's idea. The modern postal system was born.

▲ The first ever stamp, the Penny Black, made sending a letter much easier.

The Team

Just imagine what life would be like without the post. Almost everyone depends on it – but not just for keeping in touch with friends and relatives. Businesses also rely on the post to deliver letters, documents and bills.

Just like in Roman times, when messengers passed letters to other messengers, today's modern post office works like a relay race. Letters have to move quickly from one stage to the next in order to get to their destination on time. Only teamwork can make this happen.

King Edward Sorting Office

In this book we are going to see how the post office workers at King Edward Sorting Office, London, work together as a team to sort and deliver the post. The King Edward Sorting Office is one of the biggest sorting offices in Britain. Twenty-four hours a day, seven days a week, there are 2,850 people working in the building on three shifts, processing almost 12 million letters a week.

▲ **Roman messengers rode all over the empire delivering mail.**

This is the King Edward Sorting Office team. Find out about their jobs and how they work together on the relevant pages of this book. ▶

**Collection postperson
Tracey Stoker
(pages 10-12)**

**CFC operator
Alan Hunt
(pages 13-14)**

**Coder
Tony Allen
(pages 15-16)**

**Counter clerk
Sooroojlall Sookhraz
(pages 8-9)**

**Manager - Graham Thorne
(pages 24-5)**

**NP 4000 operator
Fred Leader
(pages 17-18)**

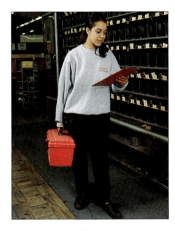

**Engineer
Michelle White
(pages 26-7)**

**Delivery postperson
Robbie Robinson
(pages 22-3)**

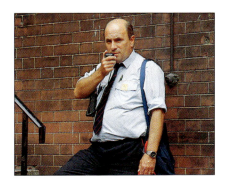

**Manual sorter
Sophie Hanmore
(pages 19-21)**

The Counter Clerk

When you go into a post office you will be helped by a counter clerk. The counter clerk doesn't just sell stamps. There are many other services that are part of the job.

At the counter

Every day each counter clerk collects a tray and a large book of stamps from the post office safe. The counter clerk places the tray on the counter in front of a window 'position'. The tray contains all the money that will be used while serving customers throughout the day.

People visit the post office for many reasons. Some may want to buy stamps or send large parcels that cannot fit into a post-box. Many senior citizens come to collect their pensions. People also come to the post office to buy television licences and tax discs for cars.

▲ While Sooroojlall is serving customers at the front counter each day, thousands of letters are being sorted by other members of the team in the same building.

▲ A customer buying stamps from the counter clerk.

Sooroojlall Sookhraz
❝ I enjoy my job because I get to meet so many people each day. ❞

The counter clerk keeps a record of everything he or she does on a computer. At the end of the day the computer record is checked. This is to make sure that the right amount of money is in the tray and the correct number of stamps left in the book before they are put back into the safe.

Getting the stamp bug

Stamp collecting, or philately, is the most popular hobby in the world. Most large post offices have a philatelic desk where collectors can buy any new stamps issued that year or first-day covers. A first-day cover is an envelope which has been postmarked on the very first day a stamp comes out.

'Poste restante'

People who are travelling in a foreign country and don't know where they will be staying can ask family and friends to send them letters to the city they are visiting, marked 'poste restante'. This is French for 'waiting mail'. Their mail will be kept in the city's main post office until they collect it.

Fact-file
- In Britain, the paper used for stamps is made from replanted Iberian Eucalyptus trees.
- There are nearly 4 million stamp collectors in Britain.
- The youngest designer of a postage stamp was just five years old, the oldest was ninety-one years old. Before any new stamp goes on sale, the King or Queen has to approve its design.

The Collection Postperson

Every day, millions of people throughout Britain post letters and parcels. All this mail has to be collected and brought back to the sorting offices as quickly as possible. This is the job of the collection postmen and women.

Emptying the post-boxes

Before going out on a collection route, called a 'walk', the postperson goes to the van depot to get the ring of keys which unlock all the post-boxes on the route. He or she then loads some empty postbags into the back of the van, checks the tyres and oil and sets off.

▲ The collection postperson, Tracey Stoker, takes a van from the depot to go on her collection route.

Tracey Stoker
' The best thing about my job is being out on the road – I really enjoy all the driving I have to do. '

▲ The letters collect in a wire cage inside the post-box. They are emptied into a postbag through an opening at the bottom of the cage.

Each collection postperson follows the same route every day, stopping off at all the post-boxes. Each time the boxes are emptied the tablet number is changed. This tells people when the next collection will be.

In London and other large towns and cities the collection postmen and women also pick up mail from large offices on their routes.

Some companies, like the Bank of England in London, may have as many as fifteen sacks of mail to be collected every day. Back at the sorting office, the postperson unloads all the bags of mail from the van into large baskets, or skips, which then go to be sorted.

▲ Back at the sorting office, the full postbags are either unloaded into skips or passed straight to the CFC operator to be sorted.

Fact-file
- A large sorting office can have as many as 120 collection postpeople.
- Postmen and women still call their collection route the 'walk', even though nowadays most of it is done by van rather than on foot.
- Unlike other vehicles, post office vans can usually park where they like without getting a parking ticket!

The CFC Operator

The skiploads of letters and parcels are taken straight to the CFC operator, who prepares them for sorting.

The CFC

The Colour Facing Canceller (CFC) turns the letters round so that all the stamps face out. It also prints the postmark on every stamp. This is called cancelling because it means the stamps cannot be used again.

How it works

The bags of collected mail are opened and any packages or very large envelopes are taken out.

1. A conveyor belt takes the letters up into a huge drum. The drum rotates (turns round and round). This removes any bits of elastic bands, paper clips, or even sweet papers that might have got caught up with the letters.

Fact-file

• The CFC machine can process 30,000 letters an hour. A counter on top of the machine keeps a check on the number of letters going through.
• The CFC machine is made in Japan. It costs £120,000.

The operator, Alan Hunt, at the control panel of the enormous CFC machine. ▼

Alan Hunt
❝ I have to act quickly to stop the CFC machine when I hear the buzzer warning me that something has got stuck. ❞

2. Each letter is then squeezed between two fast-moving belts and raced through the machine. Light sensors can tell where the stamp is on the envelope. The machine turns each letter so that the stamp is in the top right-hand corner.

3. Then the letters move into the cancelling section. A postmark, with the name of the sorting office, the time and the date, is printed over the stamp.

4. The machine can also tell whether the letter has a first- or second-class stamp. It does this by checking the amount of a chemical, called phosphorus, on the stamp. First-class stamps have phosphorus all over, while second-class stamps have a single line of phosphorus.

5. The boxes, or pods, full of letters now go to be coded and then sorted.

▲ While the operator is at the control panel at the front of the CFC machine, another worker checks the letters that have been through the machine and are stacked in the pods.

Red alert
Sometimes letters get blocked in the machine or even break open. If this happens a buzzer sounds. By looking at a control panel the CFC operator can see exactly where the fault is and fix it as quickly as possible.

◀ No time to lose – the pods, full of letters that have been postmarked and cancelled, are passed to the coder.

The Coder

The postcode for an address is a series of letters and numbers which tell the post office the city or town, postal district and street where a letter or parcel should go.

Remember the postcode

The coder sits at a coding machine, which looks very like a typewriter. A row of letters passes along in front of him or her. The coder types the postcode of each letter into the machine, which automatically prints a line of tiny blue dots on the front of the envelope.

▲ Coders, like Tony Allen, have to concentrate very hard to make sure that the correct postcodes are typed.

Tony Allen ❜ My job is quite difficult because I have only a few seconds to read the postcode and type in the correct code on my keyboard. ❜

◀ Lightning speed is needed to code the letters as they pass in front of the coder.

15

If a letter doesn't have a postcode, the code for the nearest big town is typed instead. The coder can find these in a book which is kept beside the coding machine.

Fact-file
● Coders work very fast. The best can code over 3,000 letters an hour.
● The tiny blue dots contain phosphorus. They can be 'read' by the light sensor inside the automatic sorting machines.

▲ Sometimes, letters get jammed in the coding machine or the machine breaks down. Whenever there is a problem with the coding machine the coder asks the engineer (see pages 26–7) to fix it.

The NP 4000 Operator

The NP 4000 is the most up-to-date automatic sorting machine. It reads the tiny blue dots that the coding machine has printed on each envelope and sorts them into their delivery areas. Just one NP 4000 operator can do the work that once took a team of manual sorters.

Automatic sorting

The NP 4000 operator collects the letters from the coder. He or she wheels them over to the machine on huge trolleys, called 'cakestands'.

Then the letters are placed on the 'jigger'. This is a machine that vibrates (moves up and down very quickly) to separate the bundles of letters.

At this stage he or she makes sure that there are no large or flimsy packages that could clog up the machine.

▲ Fred Leader operates the NP 4000 automatic sorting machine.

Fred Leader
❝ The NP 4000 is very noisy when it is sorting the letters. ❞

◀ The coded letters are taken off the coding machines and stacked on to the 'cakestands', ready to be sorted by the NP 4000 machine.

The letters are now ready for the NP 4000 machine. The operator presses the green button and the machine starts rolling. Each letter is passed through rollers. Light sensors read the tiny blue dots and each letter is sent to the correct stack on the sorting shelves on the machine. In just a few minutes hundreds of letters can be sorted into neat stacks for each destination.

The operator bundles each stack and adds a sticker showing the destination area. All the bundles of coded and sorted letters are then sent to the delivery area of the sorting office.

Fact-file

- Each NP 4000 costs £130,000.
- 35,000 letters can race round the machine every hour.

The letters for each postal district are bundled together with an elastic band and labelled with a sticker. ▶

The Manual Sorter

▲ The manual sorters, like **Sophie Hanmore (front)**, have to work carefully and quickly.

Some mail cannot be sorted by machines. Large letters and parcels have to be sorted by hand. This is the job of the manual sorter.

Sorting by hand

The manual sorting area is made up of rows of little boxes called pigeon-holes. Each one is for a different postal district. There are also boxes for mail that is going to places outside the city and others for mail going abroad.

The manual sorter reads the address and postcode on each letter and puts it in one of the boxes. As each box fills up it is emptied into a sack.

Sophie Hanmore
" We don't spend all our time doing sorting because it can get boring sometimes. We often get moved about to do different jobs in the building. "

Each pigeon-hole is labelled with the names or codes of the different postal districts.

Mail for areas outside London is separated into different districts and dropped down a chute to the post office underground train (see page 28).

Mail for the local delivery area is sorted again by hand into different streets ready for the postmen and women to deliver on their 'walks'.

A bag of sorted mail being dropped down the chute leading to the underground 'Mail Rail'. ▶

◀ Parcels of all shapes and sizes are sorted into big sacks, called skips. Each skip is labelled with a different postal district.

Fact-file

• Sorting post for the London area is called IPS, meaning Inward Primary Sorting. Sorting post for the rest of the country is OPS, or Outward Primary Sorting.

• It takes two weeks to be trained as a manual sorter. After the training period each manual sorter is tested and if they do not get every letter into the correct boxes they cannot keep the job.

The Delivery Postperson

▲ The delivery postperson, Robbie Robinson, sorting the mail for the 'walk' into a frame.

The delivery postperson's job is to deliver mail to homes and businesses along a particular route, or 'walk'.

On the 'walk'

6.00 a.m. The delivery postperson arrives at the sorting office and picks up a sack of mail for his or her route.

6.30 a.m. Sorts the mail for the 'walk' into a frame. A frame is a box with different pigeon-holes for every building on the 'walk'.

Robbie carries a walkie-talkie radio with him on his 'walk' so that he can contact the sorting office if there are any problems delivering the mail. ▼

7.00 a.m. Takes the mail from the frame and places it into the delivery bag in the order that it will be delivered.

8.15 a.m. Goes to the van depot.

8.30 a.m. Begins 'walk'. The delivery postperson takes each bundle of letters out of the delivery bag as he or she arrives at that street or building. Then the street number or name is checked before delivering the letter or parcel.

9.30 a.m. Returns to sorting office.

10.00 a.m. Breakfast.

10.30 a.m. Starts to get everything ready for the second delivery.

11.30 a.m. Sets out on second delivery.

12.45 p.m. Finishes second delivery.

1.30 p.m. Finishes work and heads for home.

◀ The letters Rowena is delivering to this house in London may have come from anywhere in the country, or the world! Because of teamwork in the post office most letters and parcels reach their destination quickly and safely.

The Manager

▲ The manager, Graham Thorne, checking a report. It is the manager's job to make sure that the whole team in the sorting office work together with as few problems as possible.

The manager is in charge of everything that goes on in the building. It is the manager's job to make sure that the whole system of processing the mail in the sorting office goes smoothly.

The manager's day

Every day as soon as the manager arrives in the office, he or she reads the reports from the past twenty-four hours. These tell him or her how many letters have been processed and whether there have been any problems. With over 3,200 people (including cooks and cleaners) working in one building, problems are bound to happen. It is the manager's job to make sure these are sorted out.

The manager also checks to see if the cost of running the sorting office is keeping within the budget which has been set. This is very important as it costs a lot of money to run a sorting office like the King Edward office.

Testing times

Occasionally a 'test' letter is sent through the post to make sure it reaches its destination on time and without being bent or damaged.

Every day the manager has a meeting with the supervisors of each section to check that everything is running smoothly. ▼

Fact-file

● The sorting office works non-stop. The manager sometimes stays overnight in the office so that he or she can talk to the staff on the night-shift.

The Engineer

Much of the work in a sorting office is done by machines. But machines sometimes break down. It is the job of the engineers to be ready to fix them at any time, day or night.

Fixing the equipment

Every engineer has to know exactly how all the machines in the sorting office work. When a new machine is brought into service, the engineers are given a few days training to make sure they understand how it operates.

▲ The engineer, Michelle White, can be called on to fix a broken machine anywhere in the building – so she carries her toolbox with her at all times.

▲ The engineer checks through her list of jobs for the day with the manager.

Michelle White

" Being an engineer, I'm a bit of a nuisance at home. Whenever we buy a new machine for the house, I always want to take it to bits to see how it works. "

The engineers always try to spot problems before they happen. Every day they clean all the machines and check that the conveyor belts and rollers are working properly. A machine only has to stop for a few minutes before the letters and parcels start piling up. It is the engineer's job to get the machine operating again as quickly as possible.

As well as the coding and sorting machines, a large sorting office has many delivery vans and lorries. These also have to be looked after by the engineers in the sorting office's own garage.

▲ When there is a problem with the sorting machine, it is the job of the engineer to get it working again as soon as possible.

Fact-file
- It takes three years to train as an engineer in the post office. Most of the training is done 'on the job'.

Moving the Mail

Every hour, sackloads of post leave the sorting office to be delivered to addresses all around the country. It is up to a whole network of post office workers to make sure that these letters get to homes and businesses on time.

Going underground

Even London's traffic-clogged streets cannot hold up the mail. Twenty-five metres under the city the post office has its very own underground railway. The 'Mail Rail' links the eight main sorting offices in the capital. It also speeds letters and parcels that are going elsewhere in the country, or abroad, to Paddington and Liverpool Street stations. There are no drivers or guards on this railway. It has been completely automatic since it first opened in 1927.

On the right tracks

Most of the thousands of letters that the post office delivers across the country every day go by train for at least part of their journey. Special trains are used. These are called Travelling Post Offices, or TPOs.

The TPOs are like mini sorting offices inside. On board, as the train crosses the country, a team of manual sorters prepare the post for delivery the moment it arrives at its destination.

The most famous TPOs are the 'Down Special' which travels between London and Glasgow and the 'Up Special' which goes from Glasgow to London, every night.

▲ The underground 'Mail Rail' trains are automatic – they don't need drivers.

Fact-file

- TPOs travel 12 million kilometres every year, the same distance as fifteen trips to the moon and back.
- Every year, 450 million letters are sorted on the move in TPOs.
- 'Mail Rail' takes just thirteen minutes to cross London.

Air mail

Many letters travel the country by air. The post office has its own fleet of aircraft. Some of the airports they land at are quite small. Air mail going overseas is usually carried in the cargo holds of passenger aircraft en route to those countries.

By sea

Ships are also used to carry mail to the many islands off the coast of Scotland. For the final part of the journey, some letters and parcels to the Scottish Isles are taken by rowing boat. A hovercraft takes letters to the Isle of Wight from Portsmouth on the south coast.

Bags of sorted mail being loaded from delivery vans on to a post office aeroplane. ▼

Glossary

budget The total amount of money available to spend.

'cakestands' Trolleys which are used to carry stacks of letters.

CFC The Colour Facing Canceller is the machine that separates letters and stamps on the postmark so that the stamps cannot be used again.

conveyor belt A strip of fabric or plates of metal driven by rollers which carry objects from one point to another.

destination The end of a journey.

first-day cover A cover, usually an envelope, postmarked on the first day a stamp comes out.

light sensors Special machines which can 'read' information or codes printed with light-reflective chemicals, such as phosphorus.

mailcoaches The vehicles used to deliver the mail across Britain in the eighteenth and nineteenth centuries.

night-shift The time when people work during the night.

NP 4000 The machine that sorts letters into delivery areas.

Penny Black The first stamp issued in Britain. It was coloured black and cost a penny.

philately Another word for stamp collecting.

phosphorus A chemical which reflects light.

'poste restante' The postal system used around the world which enables visitors to collect mail when they are in a foreign country.

postmark The mark which is printed on a letter by a CFC machine. It tells you the name of the sorting office, the date and the time it was printed.

tablet number The number on a post-box which tells you when the next collection will be.

'test' letter A letter sent through the post to check that letters are arriving on time and in good condition.

'walk' The name postmen and women give to their collection or delivery routes.

Books to read

First Post: from Penny Black to present day by Peter Davies (Quiller Press, 1990)
Focus on Stamps by Michael Biggs (Hamlyn, 1993)
History of British Post by Nance Fyson (Young Library, 1992)
The Post Office Project Book by Jean Barrow (Hodder and Stoughton, 1992)

Useful Addresses

If you would like to find out more about the post office or stamp collecting you can write to the following:

National Postal Museum
King Edward Building
King Edward Street
London EC1A 1LP

The British Library Philatelic Collection
Great Russell Street
London WC1B 3DG

Titles in the series
Building Site
Fire Service
Hospital
Newspapers
Police Service
Post Office

Series Editor: Geraldine Purcell
Series Designer: Loraine Hayes
© Copyright 1994 Wayland (Publishers) Limited

First published in 1994 by Wayland (Publishers) Limited
61 Western Road, Hove, East Sussex BN3 1JD, England.

British Library Cataloguing in Publication Data
Perry, Philippa
Post Office. – (Teamwork Series)
1. Title 11. Gibbs, Stephen 111. Series
383

ISBN 0 7502 1097 4

DTP design by Loraine Hayes Design
Printed and bound in Italy by Rotolito Lombarda S.p.A.

Stamp Bug Club
Freepost
Northampton NN3 1BR
(specially for young collectors, the Stamp Bug Club has more than 70,000 members).

Index

Acknowledgements

The authors and publisher wish to thank the management
and staff at the King Edward Sorting Office, London, who
co-operated in the making of this book.

Picture acknowledgements

All the photographs in this book were provided by Andrew
Perris, APM Studios, except for the following: Mary Evans
Picture Library 6; The Post Office 4–5, 5, 28–9 (both);
Wayland Picture Library 4 (bottom).